GRAVITY
Poems
1993-2013

Crystal Jenkins Woods

Copyright© Crystal Jenkins Woods, 2014

Copyright Cover Art© Leigh Van Duzer, 2014

Copyright Design© Melissa Dickson, 2014

Copyright Author Photo© Natasha Stansel, 2014

Printed in the United States of America

All Rights Reserved

Library of Congress Control Number: 2013922333

ISBN: 9780985770341

Gravity, by Crystal Jenkins Woods

Published by Summerfield Publishing, New Plains Press

PO Box 1946

Auburn, AL 36831-1946

Newplainspress.com

for Eric

Acknowledgements

Love and thanks to my husband, parents, family, and friends for decades of support and encouragement. And to K and C, my best works.

Thanks to Donna for "Red." And for everything else.

To editor Julia Bouwsma and to all the former CSU workshop members now all over the country (Abby E. Murray, Beth Spencer, Scott Wilkerson, Charish Roderick, Noreen Lape, Diana Riser)—your feedback on these poems is much appreciated. Thank you all.

Thanks to Hambidge Center Creative Residency Program and to Columbus State University's Faculty Center Writing Bootcamp for the time and space to write.

"Isis," "First Language," "Outmaneuvered," "Last Night I Went to Dinner," "Estate Sale," and "Poem Fragments" (originally titled "Poems in Outline") first appeared in *Arden*.

"What a Porno Won't Show" first appeared in *Alligator Juniper*.

"Bridge," "Haircut," "Red," "5 April 94," "Kin" and "S.M.O (1961-1991)" first appeared in *The Eclectic*.

Cover Art

The cover art is by Leigh Van Duzer, a Philadelphia-based artist whose work has been shown internationally, including galleries in New York, Washington DC, Philadelphia and Paris. In her photographic work, she combines images of natural and man-made structures to compare systems and methods of building. The cover image "Geysers" pairs the micro with the macro, showing a symmetrical biological form with a mountain in Yosemite National Park.

Contents

I
Gravity	13
New Year's Eve	14
Saturday on St. Christopher Street	15
Yellow	17
Naming Storms	18
Starter	19

II
What a Porno Won't Show	23
Five Seconds on a Down Elevator	24
Light, Smoke, Warmth	25
Returning Home after Nine Days Traveling Alone	26
Haircut	27
Bridge	28
Red	30
Gemini	31
Lavender Mist	32
Sphinx	33

III
Hambidge Ghazal	37
Poem Fragments	38
Modern Haiku Sequence	39
Play	40
Kin	41
Draft Conferences	42
Ictus Women	43

IV
Estate Sale	46
Time and the Janka Scale	47
Eel	48
Yard Girl	49
5 April 94	50
Isis	51

First Language   52
On Mondrian's Grave   53
Outmaneuvered   54
S.M.O. (1961-1991)   55
Gone   57

V
Yard Sale   60
On Passing out During My Son's Blood Test   61
Last Night I Went to Dinner   62
Kindergarten   63
Tuesday Afternoon, October   64

I.

"The ending is nearer than you think, and it is already written. All that we have left to choose is the correct moment to begin."
~Alan Moore,
V for Vendetta

"Go on till you come to the end; then stop."
~Lewis Carroll,
Alice's Adventures in Wonderland

GRAVITY

Gravity

We make our way out
by growing heavy enough
to drop like a stone
through a seam
in the bottom of a sack.
We work against its constant pull
to sit upright, to roll
around the living room.

It wants us to be still
to appreciate its commitment,
day and night without faltering,
but we want redgold afternoons
dirtbikes and backyard ramps,
our legs pumping
the length of the block
for one weightless second.

It doesn't understand
our piddling, our ambitions,
the friction of shoes
thickening callouses,
the friction of treads
scraping carpets bald,
hard rubber soles worn slick
on sidewalks, cartilage
rubbed to slivers like old soap.

Its insistence rounds our middles
into planets, stoops our frames.
It grows so tired of waiting
it trips us on the stairs.

New Year's Eve

The house is bare again, the yard
still peopled with glowing effigies,
constellations of colored lights,
the whole day an anteroom
where we doze in the tv's flicker,
strands of tinsel spangling the carpet.
The kids think up resolutions,
but introspection turns me wrongside out
like a Christmas sweater, familiar patterns
strange and tangly in reverse.

Old friends call from corners they've drifted to.
There's *Marco* in their voices, and my laugh
in the receiver says *Polo, Polo*—a kind of reckoning.
Kids circle sparklers in the grass,
oblivious to the jack-o-lantern by the steps,
its black mouth caving in. At midnight
they blare car horns long past what's reasonable,
as if this din could really be a beginning.
But I know tomorrow will look like today
strewn with confetti. Even now I feel the years
lingering at the edge of the yard
like stooped old men laboring to breathe.

Saturday on St. Christopher Street

It must have taken all night
this miracle: a corridor
of crepe paper streamers all the way down
our street. Both sides. It wound
around trees and sagged between them
zigzagging to spiral up
mailbox posts, loose ends trilling
in the breeze, the entire block doused
in swashes of pink, lavender, gold,
crimson, aqua, orange.

Neighbors stood and puzzled,
fingers looped through coffee mugs.
Some suspected the renters,
who might be in a fraternity. Others
checked phones for holidays or parades
or called friends on other streets.

But we tired of speculation
and the lawn chairs came out
and the cameras and dogs
and kids on skateboards.
Across the street men gathered
around a red mower.
One toddler would not be
diverted, his fat fists pulling off
bright bits of crepe that must've looked
like candy. Then kids on bikes
burst through the swooshy streamers,
pulverizing them into
technicolor nuisance,
like New Years confetti
after midnight.

We pulled it down, heaping it
on curbs, toted in
lawn chairs and drew baths
for tye-dyed children,
went about the day. But for weeks

lengths of streamer lingered
in branches, whipped
from mailboxes, trailed out
from the handlebars of bicycles
where small, stained fingers
had tied them on. Arriving late
from football games or rising early,
we hoped to catch someone
attempting it again.

Even months later, we'd
gather in front of the vacant
house where rain
and sopping blobs of crepe paper
stained the sidewalk
like church windows.
We went for updates,
to offer theories

but mostly for the sheer delight
of remembering it:
Streamers. Saturday.
St. Christopher Street.

Yellow

I hate its relentless smiling,
the politician's wife
the cheerleader on TV
beating the air with pom-poms.

It's fever and pus, it's the wallpaper
that drove that woman mad,
the color, yes, of cowards,
of dead winter weeds,
week-old bruises, pollen
and piss, iodide and jaundice. It's
my mother's tacky sundress

in the church pew
her blonde head shushing me
then cursing at my father
all the way home. It's the gold
band he left on the dresser
that I discovered
in a shaft of early sunlight.

Naming Storms

A tornado whips up like *that*,
quick as the wispy funnel your kid made
spinning a marble in a bottle of water, the storm
an instant omnivore hungry for library books,
sheetrock, livestock, heirlooms, swaths of trees.
Minutes before, only rain. Minutes after,
we crawl from closets, the horror nameless
even as it whirls its hell toward other towns.

But a hurricane we see coming.
We witness its birth on television,
its milestones noted by every scrolling banner,
its distant churning a certainty
we can dread. By the time we
strip shelves of batteries and plywood,
it lumbers ashore, blowing palm trees inside-out
like cheap umbrellas. These storms we know.
We name them after those who hurt us most.

Starter

A common recipe using ... starter suggests using one cup (240 ml) of it to make [friendship] bread, keeping one cup to start a new cycle, and giving the remaining cups to friends.   —Wikipedia entry

No matter how sincerely
you smile over coffee,
how often you model selflessness,
I can never give you all of me.
It must seem cruel to always find
a divot in your slice of sweet bread,
one fewer raisin than expected,
bare spots in the icing to puzzle over.

But if I had to, I could enter
my secret kitchen
(the only room left standing
after the floods the bankruptcy
the breakups the funeral dirge)
could make myself again
from these withholdings
replenish what's gobbled away

or if the grief is yours, I could
sit with you at my table
and send you home with a Mason jar
bubbling.

II.

"The easiest kind of relationship for me is with ten thousand people. The hardest is with one."
-Joan Baez

"To understand how any society functions you must understand the relationship between the men and the women."
-Angela Davis

What a Porno Won't Show

For the record, there is nothing more hopeful,
nothing more adventurous, than a penis.
Right now men in every country swing out leg casts
like the stiff pencil-leg of a drawing compass
and lean, one hand on the nightstand, into flesh.
Or give up and get in however they can,
clumsy couplings both will laugh about
but neither will request again.
At this second, naked women oozing
with poison ivy grin sheepishly at partners
up for the challenge, who plan out
finger and toe holds and begin their ascent.

One man remembers hiking the slopes
of his wife's swollen belly two straight summers
while she smiled from the horizon,
a sun about to crest. Another recalls
a mute girl from senior English
who beneath him smelled like warm caramel,
whose deft red nails etched into him
the first poem he ever got the gist of.

Five Seconds on a Down Elevator

The sudden assault of his piney cologne
traps her in the woodpaneled corner,

drops her into
Christmas morning:
a real tree in the study,
a new fake father,
ugly black roller skates.

Between 11 and 10
she can take no more.
She turns and hisses,
"I wanted the pink ones."

Light, Warmth, Smoke

Whatever glittered around her
welcomed the traveler in me,
her face an inn with windows aglow.
It lit the dashboard from the bar
to her front door draped
with Christmas lights
where she kissed me hard

and we fell inside, fingers and knees pulling me
on her poster bed, blood surging,
warm urge of eons guiding me in. After,
her dark bedroom spun me to sleep
while through windowpanes
the porch lights blinked
galaxies onto her hair.

But all I took for light was smoke.
I dress in the judgment of her cigarette.
She flicks ashes on my shoes.
I find my keys in a bowl of fake fruit.
Out on the porch the strands of spangles
become lightless plastic beads, and I
a traveler again.

Returning Home After Nine Days Traveling Alone

I can't even tell you
how happy my husband was.

What we did that first hour
was unspeakable.

Haircut

in the mirror
my head floats
disembodied
above a spotted smock
so still in the chair
as scissors
whick around my chin

eight inches of brown gone
and two years
and one lover

used to sweep those waves aside
to kiss my shoulders
fingers tangled
and arms and legs
heart free and wafting
I can touch the absence
that scissors leave

and this time I will
walk out weightless
leaving you
in dead wet curls

Bridge

I.

Some would believe it, would think I
fell asleep, let the sleek beast have its head
and arced, right-kiltered, into concrete.

I'd done it before, almost.
The encore done, I'd started home
giving all the lanes
the pleasure of my tires
head dropping and dropping,
jerking awake in a Waffle House
far from anywhere
drool on the counter.

What no one would believe
is that tiny double lines on a plastic stick
a vulgar pink centerstripe
could be enough to make me
hold that pedal down.
I prayed and waited
O to be washed in the blood
but nothing. nothing.

II.

In my headlights the bridge supports
are thick and strong, Atlases
holding up the road above,
arms that would save me
if I veered toward them,
and for the first time I don't want to do it

don't want to dodge the airbag
don't want to feel my flesh peeling easy
like tangerine skin
don't want to punish us
for loving each other.

I put the car in gear and drive
toward your apartment,
the bridge raw and red
in my rearview.

Red

Toward the end she slobbers
it was her fault
but he hears nothing
not even her head splitting
on the corner of the cabinet,
sadclownface sliding tileward
wild hair, black tears
and blood   blood
pinkish on her clothes,
mouth vivid

Between his hands
her throat gurgles a frenzied plea

shattered teeth recall the sand
salty lips long for the sea
for the peace of sink
                    ing
                         eas
                    y

Afterwards
he drives downtown,
the dashboard singing
there is love, there is love

At the redlight
he eases the car still
and looks up
waiting

obedient

Gemini

I knew her from Chemistry, which is to say
I knew little—she texted through class,
hated waitressing, drank coffee like a fiend.

On the quad one Tuesday we passed each other,
her gaze strangely blank, a glacier
or a locked gray door without a peephole,
the proportions her face drifting tectonically—
the twin, I learned, of the one in my class.

I had forgotten that sensation of her-but-not
until this morning when I came in softly
with bagels and a newspaper, and you said softly
into a phone I wasn't on the other end of, *I love you.*

Lavender Mist
National Gallery of Art, Washington D.C.

After museum-goers dwindle
and schoolchildren in matching shirts
file onto waiting busses, after judiciously,
deliciously saving it for last,
I step forward and eye it
where it lazes along a wall.
It leans in, marbley patterns magnified,

and I go back to a middle school dance
with a dark-haired, square-shouldered boy
in sharp cologne and a pink oxford shirt
he wore through science lab and hot dog lunch,
through recess puddles and leaky pen,
that I might swoon at dusk in his presence.

A black-clothed docent, like a schoolmarm,
taps hard on my shoulder, lowering
her forearm just before
I murmur in his ear.

Sphinx

By the time she says she's leaving,
the scout has been dispatched
to another city, one with coffee shops
art museums   good shopping
a place where you are not, where

you never held her on the balcony
while the city filled up with stars,
never latched the clasp of a charm bracelet
that tinked when she reached for you,
where you did not wake to find the dog snoring
between you in the sheets and her

awake, staring a hole through the ceiling.
By the time you say we need to talk about this,

the scout slips back into her body
and suddenly on her breath
the aroma of hazelnut, on her skin a perfume
you can't name, could not afford.

III.

"Language is very powerful. Language does not just describe reality.
Language creates the reality it describes."
~Desmond Tutu

"Painting is silent poetry,
and poetry is painting that speaks."
~Plutarch

Hambidge Ghazal

Seven hours of solitude, eight bottles of Blue Moon;
I lean over the koi pond to flirt with the moon.

What has insomnia, wanderlust, and one silver eye?
A car with one headlight, some kin of the moon.

The crickets' lonely fiddling brings me back to you,
how we listened from the balcony on our honeymoon.

Each insect in my yard becomes a realist at dusk
and taps at my widow instead of the moon's.

Silly me, packing shorts and sandals for summertime,
but this house in the woods is as cold as the moon.

Poem Fragments

Sometimes when I come down the hall
with a basket of laundry
or sag in an elevator after work,
one will manifest, musty, insistent,
half-membered. I don't look.
I know what it wants.

Modern Haiku Sequence

first green morning . . .
to my eaves
sparrows return

spring thunder rattles windows—
small son
takes my hand

***

summer afternoon . . .
a bee's droning
bores us to sleep

summer dusk—
I wish mosquitoes
were more like fireflies

***

autumn sunset—
can we endure
this much red?

your leaving
did not cause my tears . . .
it was the burning leaves

***

distant mountains
vanish in fog—
lonely winter morning

crossing fields in snowdrifts—
my dog's black tail
guides me home

Play

This poem assumes I want to play.
It stands on the lawn on a Saturday morning
chucking periods, periods, periods at my window
until I emerge in sock feet. The ball and glove
I can see, but its pockets bulge
with mysteries—coins, maybe,
but I hope for candy.
When it takes off toward the park,
I slip on sneakers and give chase.
I can almost smell the infield grass,
almost taste the peppermint.

Kin
(for B.J. Jenkins)

Your last name
does not resonate
the timbre of drums
does not speak
of palms dripping
does not throb

it is prim
like pointy shoes
and translucent
teacups

the flesh of my fathers' thighs
stole your name
and gave you mine
a high-buttoned collar
that burns like rope braid
we tear at our throats

sugar sister burnt to caramel
by flaming crucifix
is this my price for heritage
to know you claim the zebra kin
not me?

Draft Conferences, English 1102

For a week they've come,
my office a checkpoint.
Their faces show miles run alone
down topics where no one would follow
across the raw terrain of poems,
through the crossfire dialogue of plays.

They've seen things and show me
two poems that feel the same,
like fraternal towns on different hills
and they the runner between.
Some run through tombs,
who bring news of Emily and Sylvia,
who don't seem to mind
the cobwebs trailing from their hair.

Ictus Women

I.

Blanc. Blanca.
Bel. Bella.
The first a default,
the simple perfect original,
the second a lesser version
used for beasts of burden—
extra vowels, extra chores,
extra bodies inside theirs.

At the end of a line of poetry
these words scan
masculine or feminine
strong or weak
his words, her words,
unequal words
or else there would be
only one.

II.

Ictus:
the angle of an axe handle
whose blade splits
the kitchen table, the taut
rigging of a clipper ship,
the slant of a plow blade
as it rips through earth,
the word itself
a barb on the tongue.

Breve:
the curved underside of a breast,

a shallow puddle, the sagging shape
of an apron filled with apples,
a receptacle, a round place
where babies curl inside,
the half-moons fingernails leave
in the headboard.

III.

My grandmother
raised six girls alone,
leaned ictus-like over a sink
scrubbing rich folks' laundry
with bleach-etched hands.
Her girls ate their suppers,
each slanted fork an ictus.

Mother was a sitter at ten,
a waitress at fifteen. At fifty-four
she earned a master's degree,
her keyboard clicking
iambically

just another Ictus Woman
bracing against the wind.

IV.

"Since the day of my birth, my death began its walk.
It is walking toward me, without hurrying."
~Jean Cocteau

"The afternoon knows what the morning never suspected."
~ Robert Frost

Estate Sale

Those who had visited before
were put off by the lack of staging,
all the things her son didn't come for
exactly where she'd left them:
mantles sagging with dusty picture frames
the faces inside nearly obscured,
three years of *Good Housekeeping*
sliding from baskets by the chaise,
plates stacked in cupboards,
one dining room chair angled out
where she'd risen from supper
or breakfast or lunch,
a constellation of costume jewelry
glittering against a dark dresser,
stool softener by the sink.

I who didn't know her
lingered over an Oriental tea set
splashed with gold and cobalt.
"Her son brought it back
from the war" someone said,
but not which one, or why
her thumb had not rubbed white
even one gold handle.

This tea set sits in my kitchen now,
untouched by me as by her
except once, the day I bought it,
when on the last sip of pu-erh
I glimpsed, in the bottom of the cup,
the pale gray face of a geisha,
expression corpselike,
makeup thick and funereal.

How that bone
china trembled against my lips.

Time and the Janka Scale

Nothing's solid except now
this second and whatever we've tucked
into the pocket of our memory,
even the next footfall too abstract
for the fact of feet.

Everything else dry rots —
Latin declensions, piano chords,
which streets cross
in cities we moved from.

We don't realize how long it's been
until we reach back fumbling,
and all the things we neglected
crush to powder in our hands.

Eel
(to Plath's "Mirror")

I saw it flash on the surface
then dive through brackish shadows,
not a terrible fish but a sinuous
silver eel with unblinking eyes that startled me,
old woman's lipless shriveled mouth.

In the bathroom mirror
I flip damp brown hair this way and that,
tweezers poised, trying to flush it out.

Yard Girl

The neighbor girl used to wave
as I passed. Maybe I didn't notice her
once, or a few times, for now
she inches into the road
to stare me down or zing
my car with gravel.

In dreams I turn and look
into her face, which is always mine
at twelve, disappointed we never
moved to Paris, never drove a 'Vette.

In the dream I flip her off
and drive away.

5 April 94

nothing stopped the music
as the mob
drunk off your bitter brew
pushed you on to the pedestal
reluctant colossus in ripped-up jeans

nothing stopped the music
when we screamed in my car, you so loud
I couldn't hear me, couldn't feel me
and I with such conviction I forgot
you resented us all

nothing stopped the music
but the hand that wrote it,
your final heavy seconds
void of rage and growling guitars
silence before nirvana

Isis

Still, I dream of hands.

His right one gestures as the bus pulls away.
Who knew it was really goodbye?
The bus bleeds into yellow FBI slickers
turning to me with the news.
Between the creek banks he sleeps face down.
The current stirs his arms but he
          doesn't wave. I wake
     before they
tell me

why.

The Millers arrive at the police station at nine.
The mother's blue eyes soften out of focus
as her mind sweeps the country, the world, for her daughter.
The father looks past me as I talk of leads, of hope.
They leave single file, each rigid in their separate griefs.

Mrs. Bell comes by with Scott, missing two days
and rescued from a shed in Tulsa. "We bought you these."
I take the two small shapes cut from paper and
tape them on my office wall, near the many others
that flutter and curl. Reaching for me fifty fold
are my son's hands.

First Language
In memory of linguist Dr. Cheryl Wharry

Later, we speak French or English or Spanish,
willing our lips to form syllables:
Je suis ici en vacances. Mi perro es blanco y negro.
But first we spoke a common tongue,
a language of phonemes and slobbered pitches:
Da-Da-Da- Ba-BA! We invented
onomatopoeia, the sound the word.
Even years later we sometimes forget
we learned anything else.
When the bone snaps, when the
mother bears down, when the husband's
chest does not rise again,
we wail in our native tongue.

The permanence of your passing
hangs between us like a locked office door,
reminding us all we are fluent
in the language of loss.

On Mondrian's Grave
Brooklyn, New York

On the Metro, block after block
in rocking darkness, stepping off
at Cypress Hills Cemetery into grass
that grows in the shadow of his name.
Certainly he smiles at this, green now
after so much posturing.

Crosslegged, I cue up boogie woogie,
one earbud for me, the other dangling earthward
to stir his finger bones scattered now
like lengths of broken chalk. But once
those hands formed red, blue, yellow tiles
on black grids straight and sharp
as the creases in his suit pants. He listed home
his first New York evening
drunk on jazz and neon, not a Nazi in sight.

Months later, as pneumonia raged,
he became his own work:
coughing blood, pallor cyanotic
under yellow lights in that white studio,
no better abstraction than death.

Outmaneuvered

Bland Thursday:
stoplights, stale gum,
unremarkable until
a hearse arcs into the road
just ahead

and something in me
balks at this procession.

Without braking, I
veer down a side street
past the high school, past
the house with the ferns
to the four-way stop.
Two blocks down,
the black hood, the blue lights,
the yellow feeling.

At my urging the car strains
to twice the speed limit. I brake
fifty feet from the crossroads
fishtailing up to the motorcade.

I turn toward the hearse,
toward the grim, bearded face
of Charon at the wheel
and under my tongue

I taste metal.

S.M.O. (1960-1991)

you must've born them
screaming
each time knowing
it was yours alone
the men nine months gone
the appetite of thighs abated
by the throb of life between them

sticky redblue son
screaming
with you   at you
mother and child
enraged

Mother.
breeder of my 'brothers'
holder of Jack-and-Cokes
but not of baby bottles
waver from squad cars
feeder of lies
leaver. deceiver. deserter.
mother

dead of booze at thirty-one
pauper's funeral in
Sodom-by-the-Sea
a hundred miles
though you couldn't know it
from former sons
shrieking through Space Mountain
holding my parents' hands
wearing mouse ears
and my last name

it's a small world after all
it's a small world after all

small as this house feels
small as our chances for peace
small as the little boys who came to us
and will leave from us

screaming

Gone

The carnival is gone.
Men in blue jeans striped with grease
folded midway rides into impossible origami, stacked
silver-glittered kiddie cars onto trucks,
moved on to other lots in other towns.

Crows gobble popcorn on the spot
where a girl in red boots once
slipped a cotton-candied hand into her father's
and he gazed down into her face.

Now a middle-aged woman
weeps in a drive-thru across the street
and the father who doesn't recognize her
is pressing the red button on his bed,
telling the nurse who rushes in
the carnival passed by his window—
can he please, please go?

V.

"Making the decision to have a child is momentous. It is to decide forever to have your heart go walking around outside your body."
~Elizabeth Stone

"You are the closest I will ever come to magic."
~Suzanne Finnamore,
The Zygote Chronicles

Yard Sale

Sawhorse tables, flowered bedsheets
heaped with broken toys. My folks and I
are intrigued by this otherness—
scraped-up red bicycles that keep their stories,
hideous wall art, clothes that reek
of strangers' detergent, too sharp or too sweet.
We linger over power tools

and paperbacks, over spicy, mildew-speckled LPs
with hokey covers, the models' silver eyelids
fringed with fake lashes. I pause
over a box of animal-print gift bags –
"SURPRISE $1." Whatever it is, I want it
and fish a dollar from my pocket.

In the back seat as we pull away
I rip the bag and dump it:
tiny green lipsticks, tubes of lotions
named "Seduction" and "Fantasy,"
yellow-tinted liquid in a vial with
loopy letters and a stopper
that pops under my thumb. A rivulet
of perfume snakes down my forearm.
Lipstick next, a poppy color, then the lotion.
The interior is choked with my pungency,

but they just stare ahead, shadows
on green lawns flickering past,
the front seat farther away, my orange-red lips
the sun of a new world.

On Passing Out During My Son's Blood Test

[E]xisting evolutionary biological hypotheses regarding fainting are pan-mammalian; they argue that a tendency towards blood-induced faintness evolved prior to the emergence of the genus Homo and is common to all mammals.
                                        ~H. Stefan Bracha, MD

His blood was so red
it drove me out of myself,
his blown vein a purple knot.

I would like to say
because we once were connected
his panic traversed
our phantom vine, but
at anyone's blood
gravity arcs a black wave
over my head.

I come to, sweating,
a messenger just arrived
from a great distance,
cave dust clinging to my ankles.

Last Night I Went to Dinner

essays ungraded, water bill unopened,
children's socks in the kitchen floor
just where they'd dropped them
where the sitter stood and waved me out.
Laundry spilled out of the dryer
in a warm cotton avalanche,
but I escaped.

Kindergarten

Through repetition I get used to
scratching my son's name on forms
until his identity toughens and sets.
He is public: he has teachers (plural),

an assigned seat, library and lunch cards.
Under the breezeway that first afternoon
he is straighter, more. An hour later,
at Publix, he folds into a racecar buggy
and we traverse the aisles like a parade route,
a gallon of orange juice riding shotgun,
the face of every label turned to watch us pass.

At checkout his knees won't budge, his femurs
as long as the red plastic cab. I pull
him out by the arms, my fingers forceps,
his squealing drawing a small crowd,
his first-day nametag proclaiming,
My name is Carson.

The electric doors roll open and he strolls
into the afternoon, the asphalt marked with yellow
like a chalkboard.

Tuesday Afternoon, October

His fidelity has worn a bare spot
by the mailbox where at the sound
of tires on gravel he spins,
suspended, nearly, by centrifugal love.
But the schoolbus rumbles on

and the boy who would leap
from the last black step and sail
his backpack into the grass
slumps in a library carrel hours away.

From her kitchen window,
the boy's mother notes the dust cloud settling,
notes the dog's pitiful spinning vigil,
washes the same plate over again,
tells her heart *lie down, be still.*

www.ingramcontent.com/pod-product-compliance
Lightning Source LLC
Chambersburg PA
CBHW021026090426
42738CB00007B/919